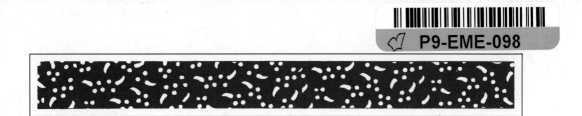

WILD ABOUT MUNCHIES

BY DOTTY GRIFFITH

BARRON'S

New York • London • Toronto • Sydney

All inquiries should be addressed to:
Barron's Educational Series, Inc.
250 Wireless Boulevard
Hauppauge, New York 11788

Library of Congress Catalog Card No. 88-8060
International Standard Book No. 0-8120-4096-1

Library of Congress Cataloging in Publication Data

Griffith, Dotty.
  Wild about munchies.

  Includes index.
  1. Snack foods. 2. Cookery. I. Title.
TX740.G724 1989   641.5'3   88-8060
ISBN 0-8120-4096-1

Design by Milton Glaser, Inc.
Color photographs by Matthew Kline
Andrea Swenson, food stylist
Francine Matalon-Degni, photo stylist
Julie Gong, prop stylist
Photo 2 opposite page 17: placemat courtesy Pottery Barn
Photo 3 opposite page 24: bowl courtesy Williams Sonoma; placemat, Pottery Barn
Photo 8 opposite page 49: bowl and plate courtesy of Pan American Phoenix
Photo 11 opposite page 64: server courtesy of Oneida

Printed and bound in Hong Kong
9012 4900 987654321

CONTENTS

INTRODUCTION

*C*all it grazing, snacking . . . call it eating little meals . . .
no matter the name, munching has replaced three squares
for many people in this country.

*If a family gets one sit-down meal together during any
given day, it's an occasion. But busy schedules, two-career
households, latchkey kids and the feeling that there's more to life
than oven pot roast and potatoes make food to be eaten while
doing something else more attractive than ever.*

*And that often is what snacking or munching is all
about. Eating while watching TV, reading, working, driving,
entertaining, celebrating a birthday, anniversary or promotion .
. . you name it and we like to do it around some dish we call a
snack.*

*Often that food can be eaten out of hand. Often it is
portable. Occasionally it is a full meal in itself.*

*More often than not, it is sweet, a treat. Sometimes it is
spicy or salty, perfect for combining with a beer, cocktails or
wine.*

*For many adults, snacking replaces mealtime. Five
"munchies" a day is what they live on. For kids, snacking is a
way to keep going and growing. Even with a well-rounded
breakfast, lunch and dinner, many kids need the extra nutrients*

supplied by snacks. Active, growing children need additional little meals during the day. Snacks don't spoil dinners; they keep the kids from starving until it's ready.

The recipes in this book are for any and all ages and many occasions. There are full meals and desserts, crunchies, savories and all manner of munchies for preparing and eating at just about any time or for any event, from watching a ballgame at home to a picnic at the stadium.

CONVERSION TABLES

The weights and measure in the lists of ingredients and cooking instructions for each recipe are in both U.S. and metric units.

LIQUID MEASURES

The Imperial cup is considerably larger than the U. S. cup. Use the following table to convert to Imperial liquid units.

AMERICAN CUP (in book)	IMPERIAL CUP (adjusts to)
¼ cup	4 tablespoons
⅓ cup	5 tablespoons
½ cup	8 tablespoons
⅔ cup	¼ pint
¾ cup	¼ pint + 2 tablespoons
1 cup	¼ pint + 6 tablespoons
1¼ cups	½ pint
1½ cups	½ pint + 4 tablespoons
2 cups	¾ pint
2½ cups	1 pint
3 cups	1½ pints
4 cups	1½ pints + 4 tablespoons
5 cups	2 pints

Note: The Australian and Canadian cup measures 250 mL and is only slightly larger than the U. S. cup, which is 236mL. Cooks in Australia and Canada can follow the exact measurements given in the recipes, using either the U. S. or metric measures.

SOLID MEASURES

British and Australian cooks measure more items by weight. Here are approximate equivalents for basic items in the book.

	U. S. Customary	Imperial
Butter	¼ cup	2 oz.
	½ cup	4 oz.
	1 cup	8 oz.
Cheese (grated)	½ cup	2 oz.
Flour (sifted)	¼ cup	1¼ oz.
	½ cup	2½ oz.
	1 cup	5 oz.
Herbs (fresh chopped)	¼ cup	¼ oz.
Meats (chopped)	1 cup	6–8 oz.
Nuts (chopped)	¼ cup	1 oz.
	½ cup	2 oz.
	1 cup	4 oz.
Raisins	¼ cup	1½ oz.
	½ cup	3 oz.
	1 cup	6 oz.
Sugar (granulated brown)	¼ cup	1¾ oz.
	½ cup	3 oz.
	1 cup	6½ oz.
Vegetables (chopped)	½ cup	2 oz.
	1 cup	4 oz.

OVEN TEMPERATURES

British cooks should use the following settings.

Gas mark	¼	2	4	6	8
Fahrenheit	225	300	350	400	450
Celsius	110	150	180	200	230

COUCH POTATO NOSHES

These are little meals for eating while watching TV or doing just about any at-home activity—such as playing bridge, poker or other games. They're also good for casual entertaining, for use as hors d'oeuvres or informal suppers.

WET FRIES

SERVES 2 TO 4

INGREDIENTS

½ package (8 ounces/230 g)
frozen French fries
1 can (10 ounces/300 g) chili
with or without beans
1 cup (240 mL) nacho cheese
sauce or 1 cup (115 g) grated
Cheddar cheese

Optional garnishes: chopped
tomatoes, sliced jalapeños,
Mexican salsa, sour cream, sliced
black olives, chopped green
chilies, sliced green onions

I believe this dish is a midwestern invention. Definitely not finger food, it is a wonderfully messy but substantial snack, best eaten with a fork and lots of napkins. It's great for assembling during commercial breaks so you don't miss a moment of your favorite thriller.

Heat French fries in oven according to package directions. Meanwhile, heat chili and cheese sauce separately. To assemble wet fries, place fries on a warm, preferably ovenproof or microwave-safe plate. Top with chili and cheese sauce or grated cheese. If using grated cheese, place plate in oven or microwave briefly to melt cheese, if desired.

Garnish as desired with any of the suggested toppings.

Variation

For a distinctly Southern variation, "White Fries," heat French fries in oven according to package directions. Crumble and brown 8 ounces (230g) bulk pork sausage over medium heat in large skillet. Drain on paper

*toweling. Pour off all but 2
tablespoons drippings. Over medium
heat, stir in 3 tablespoons flour. Stir
until smooth and cook until bubbly.
Gradually add 1½ cups (360 mL)
warm milk. Stir and heat until
thickened. Add browned sausage.
Season to taste with salt and red or
black pepper.*

*Thin slightly with water if needed,
then taste again for seasonings.
Simmer a few minutes longer. Pour
over French fries.*

FRENCH BREAD PIZZA

SERVES 2 TO 4

INGREDIENTS

2 (8-inch/20-cm) French bread
sandwich rolls
1 can (8 ounces/230 g) tomato
sauce
1 teaspoon Italian herb
seasoning
¼ teaspoon garlic salt or powder
8 ounces (230 g) crumbled
ground beef or
Italian sausage,
browned and drained
1 cup (115 g) shredded
mozzarella or Monterey Jack
cheese with jalapeños
⅓ cup (40 g) sliced ripe or green
olives
chopped fresh basil, if desired
2 to 3 tablespoons olive oil

The toppings in this recipe can vary according to mood and what you've got on hand. Pizza lovers will always want to keep a loaf in the freezer for when the urge strikes and they prefer their own pizza to one that's delivered.

Preheat oven to 425°F (215°C). Slice sandwich rolls in half lengthwise. Combine tomato sauce, Italian herb seasoning and garlic salt or powder. Spread rolls with seasoned tomato sauce. Sprinkle ground beef or sausage on each half and top with cheese and olives. Sprinkle with basil. Drizzle olive oil over pizzas. Bake open-faced for 8 to 10 minutes.

*These are simple turnover-style
sandwiches made from flour tortillas,
using the classic ingredients of a club
sandwich with a few Southwestern
touches. They can be eaten hot or at
room temperature.*

*Preheat griddle over medium heat.
Have all ingredients ready to
assemble quesadillas. Heat tortillas,
one at a time, just until soft and
pliable.*

*When each tortilla is soft, place ¼
cup (30 g) cheese on half of tortilla.
Top with a half slice of chicken.
Sprinkle desired amount of bacon
and salsa over chicken. Top with a
half slice of ham and ¼ cup (30 g)
cheese.*

*Fold over tortilla. Brush each side
lightly with butter or oil and set
aside. Repeat with remaining
tortillas until you have four half-
moon turnovers.*

*Cook tortillas over medium-high heat
2 at a time, until ingredients are
heated through and cheese is melted.
Cut each into 3 triangles.*

QUÓUCH CLUB QUESADILLAS

SERVES 4

INGREDIENTS

4 flour tortillas
2 cups (230 g) grated Cheddar
cheese
2 thin slices smoked chicken or
turkey, halved
4 slices crisp bacon, finely
crumbled (optional)
¾ cup (180 mL) chunky
Mexican-style salsa with green
chilies (optional)
2 thin slices ham, halved
butter or vegetable oil

Variation

Omit softening tortillas. Lightly butter or oil one side of each tortilla. Place 2 tortillas, buttered side down, on preheated griddle over medium heat. Sprinkle ½ cup (60 g) cheese over each tortilla. Top each with 2 pieces of chicken and half the bacon and salsa, then with 2 pieces of ham and ½ cup (60 g) cheese. Cover with remaining tortillas, buttered side up, and cook for 20 to 30 seconds, or just until bottom tortilla begins to crisp and brown. Carefully lift with spatula to check. Using spatula, gently turn each quesadilla and cook on other side until ingredients are heated through and cheese is melted, 2 to 3 minutes. Cut each into 6 wedges.

Tip

These may be cooked in advance and refrigerated. Heat, wrapped tightly in foil, at 300°F (150°C) for 20 minutes.

When these bar snacks made their way out of Buffalo, New York, several years ago, the whole country went wild for them. This is an easy method for cooking them, with a Cajun twist to the seasoning.

Preheat oven to 350°F (180°C). Remove wing tips and discard. Cut wings in half at joint. Combine butter and seasonings in microwave or in small saucepan and heat until butter is just melted. Mix well.

Dip each wing part in butter mixture to coat evenly. Arrange wings on nonstick jellyroll pan or 9 x 13-inch (22 x 33-cm) baking pan. Bake for 25 to 30 minutes or until done (juices should run clear when wings are pierced with fork).

If desired, cook wings in microwave: dip wings into butter mixture, then arrange on microwave-safe pan with rack. Cover loosely with waxed paper. Cook on high power for 7 to 12 minutes, rotating dish once. Test for doneness by piercing with a fork; wings are done when juices run clear.

HOT WINGS

SERVES 4

INGREDIENTS

20 to 24 chicken wings
(approximately 2 to 2½
pounds/900 to 1125 g)
¼ cup (60 g) butter or
margarine
2 tablespoons hot pepper sauce,
or to taste
1 tablespoon Worcestershire
sauce
1 teaspoon Old Bay Seasoning
(or any spicy seafood seasoning)
celery sticks
bottled blue cheese or ranch
dressing

Serve with celery sticks and dressing for dipping.

Variation

This relies on Italian spices for flavoring. For Italian Hot Wings, use ¼ cup (60 mL) vegetable oil or margarine, 2 tablespoons liquid red pepper sauce, 1 tablespoon Worcestershire sauce, 2 tablespoons prepared oil-free Italian salad dressing and ¼ teaspoon Italian seasoning. Combine ingredients as above and dip wings into mixture before cooking.

Opposite: French Bread Pizza (p.12)
Overleaf: Quouch Club Quesadillas (p.13)

My first experience with fried jalapeños was during my college days at the University of Texas at Austin. To get an order of torpedoes, as they were called, you had to drive far from campus to a grungy little drive-in run by an irascible proprietor who liked nothing better than to tell a person with an obviously insatiable desire for an order of six that he'd just sold the last ones to "that guy walking out the door."

Lately, with the rise of Southwestern cuisine, they're on the menus of just about every restaurant that can spell chimichanga.

Combine cornbread mix with oil and beer and mix well. Set aside for 30 minutes.

Meanwhile, prepare jalapeños. Wearing rubber gloves, make a small slit in each pepper, just large enough to carefully remove the seeds and veins. Rinse, being careful not to tear peppers. Place on paper towels to dry. Carefully fill each pepper with grated cheese. Stuff fully, but do not overstuff.

FRIED JALAPEÑOS WITH GUACAMOLE AND CHILI CON QUESO

SERVES 4

FRIED JALAPEÑOS

1 package (6 ounces/180 g) yellow cornbread mix
1 tablespoon vegetable oil
¾ cup (180 mL) beer
2 jars or cans (14-ounce/420 g) jalapeño peppers (about 24 peppers), with stems
½ cup (60 g) grated Cheddar or Monterey Jack cheese, or more if desired
vegetable oil for frying
½ cup (60 g) all-purpose flour
guacamole and/or chili con queso (see following recipes), optional

Begin heating about 3 inches of oil to 350°F (180°C). When oil is hot, roll each pepper in flour, then dip into batter, covering completely. Repeat this step, rolling peppers first in flour, then in batter to help batter adhere.

Working quickly but carefully, fry as many peppers as you can at one time without crowding the pan; peppers should float freely or they will stick together. Turn and brown on all sides, about 1 to 2 minutes; do not overcook or the cheese will ooze out and burn.

Drain on paper towels and keep warm while frying remaining peppers. Serve warm with guacamole and/or chili con queso for dipping, if desired.

Note

This batter makes enough for about 50 fried jalapeños. If that many are desired, just double the number of peppers and amount of cheese. They can be battered and frozen for frying at a later time.

Variation

Also serve tortilla chips for dipping.

To make guacamole peel and seed avocados. Mash coarsely with fork to desired consistency. Add juice, salsa and salt. Cover tightly with plastic wrap and refrigerate until serving time. Serve with tortilla chips and fried jalapeños.

To make chili con queso combine and melt cheese and tomatoes in microwave-safe dish or top of double boiler over simmering water. (To melt in microwave, place cheese in large bowl and microwave at high power 1 minute. Stir and repeat, as necessary, until cheese is melted.) Keep warm in chafing dish. Serve with tortilla chips and fried jalapeños.

GUACAMOLE

SERVES 4

INGREDIENTS

2 ripe avocados
juice of ½ lemon or lime
¼ to ½ cup (60 to 120 mL)
Mexican salsa
salt to taste

CHILI CON QUESO
(CHEESE WITH PEPPERS)

SERVES 4

INGREDIENTS

1 box (2 pounds/900 g)
processed American cheese,
cubed
1 can (10 ounces/300 g) diced
tomatoes with green chilies
or stewed tomatoes, drained
and coarsely chopped

PITA CALZONES

SERVES 4

INGREDIENTS

2 cups (230 g) shredded
provolone cheese
6 slices bacon, cooked and
crumbled, or 6 ounces (180 g)
prosciutto, chopped
½ cup (60 g) chopped,
parboiled spinach or escarole
½ teaspoon garlic salt
1 teaspoon Italian herb
seasoning
4 pita loaves
1 egg, lightly beaten with 1
tablespoon water

Much easier than true calzones, made from yeast dough, this is a couch potato's dream recipe.

Preheat oven to 350°F (180°C). Toss together cheese, bacon or prosciutto, spinach and seasonings. Cut off 1 inch (2.5 cm) of pita loaves and open pocket, being careful not to separate sides. Stuff each with equal amount of cheese mixture.

Brush inside and outside of top edge of pitas with egg and press together to seal, using picks to secure if necessary. Arrange pitas on baking sheet and brush top of each with remaining egg wash.

Bake for 15 minutes or until cheese is melted. Cool slightly, then cut in half to serve.

Variation

Use 1 cup (115 g) sliced fresh mushrooms instead of spinach.

IN THE GREAT OUTDOORS

These snacks are for taking with you on a picnic, hike or campout. They're designed to be make-ahead, portable and substantial. But don't think you have to be in the Grand Tetons to enjoy them. Treats like Pecan Banana Scones and Ham and Cheese Muffins make great breakfast take-alongs, whether it's to school or office.

PECAN BANANA SCONES

SERVES 8

INGREDIENTS

2 cups (230 g) all-purpose flour
⅓ cup (80 g) sugar
¼ teaspoon salt
1½ teaspoons baking powder
¼ cup (60 g) butter or
margarine
⅓ cup (40 g) chopped pecans
1 egg, lightly beaten
2 tablespoons milk or cream
1 cup (240 mL) mashed ripe
banana
cinnamon sugar (optional)

Of course, scones are great hot, but they also pack well for taking along on the trail. A bit of honey, jam or easily transported cream cheese or butter makes them a wonderful camper's breakfast or hiker's snack. But don't overlook the possibilities of eating these fresh out of the oven for breakfast or afternoon tea:

Preheat oven to 350°F (180°C). Lightly butter an 11-inch (28-cm) circle on a baking sheet.

Sift together flour, sugar, salt and baking powder. Cut butter into flour mixture until it is the texture of coarse meal. Add nuts and toss to mix.

Combine egg, milk and banana. Stir into dry ingredients, mixing with a fork just until a soft, sticky dough forms. Spread the dough into a 9-inch (22-cm) circle in the center of the prepared baking sheet.

Using a serrated knife, cut dough into 8 wedges. Bake for 30 to 35 minutes, or until lightly browned and a cake tester or toothpick inserted into the center comes out clean.

Place the baking sheet on a wire rack. Sprinkle tops of scones with cinnamon sugar, if desired. Cool for about 5 minutes. Transfer the scones to a wire rack to cool. Recut into wedges, if necessary. Serve warm, or cool completely and store in an airtight container or airtight wrapping.

G.O.R.P. PLUS
(GOOD OLD RAISINS AND PEANUTS PLUS POPCORN)

SERVES 4 TO 6

INGREDIENTS

1 jar (12½ ounces/375 g)
roasted peanuts*
1 box (5 oz/150 g) dark or
golden raisins, or a combination
2 quarts (2 L) plain popcorn,
salted or unsalted

*Peanuts may be oil roasted, dry roasted,
salted or unsalted, as you prefer.

This is great to take with you on the trail in small amounts. Grab a handful or two and put it in a plastic bag for your pocket. A munch along the way will do you good.

As for getting it to the campsite, put it in a large container. This stuff goes fast. Although the popcorn isn't heavy, it does take up space, so it's not something you want to backpack up on the mountain with you in any substantial quantity. Leave it at base camp.

Combine peanuts and raisins, tossing well to distribute. In a very large bowl, add popcorn in several batches to make sure ingredients are evenly distributed.

Place in airtight plastic bags or tins. Will keep fresh for a couple of days if kept from moisture.

Opposite: G.O.R.P. Plus

Throw these in a backpack for the outing's first breakfast or lunch, or pack them in the car for a meal on the road. Some box juices or aseptically packed milk cartons will keep you going on a full stomach until you get to the next truly scenic stop.

Preheat oven to 400°F (200°C). Grease cups and top surface of a 2½-inch (6-cm) muffin pan.

Mix dry ingredients in medium bowl. Add eggs, milk, and oil and mix just until blended. Fold in cheese, ham and scallions. Spoon into prepared cups, filling to the tops for oversize muffins. Bake 15 to 20 minutes or until golden brown.

Immediately transfer from pan to wire rack. Serve warm, with butter if desired.

For a complete meal, serve with green or fruit salad, or with vegetable crudités or fresh fruit eaten out of hand.

HAM AND CHEESE MUFFINS

MAKES 12 LARGE MUFFINS

INGREDIENTS

1 cup (115 g) unbleached flour
1 cup (115 g) yellow cornmeal
2 tablespoons sugar
1 tablespoon baking powder
½ teaspoon salt
¼ teaspoon garlic powder
¼ teaspoon dry mustard
2 eggs, lightly beaten
1 cup (240 mL) milk
¼ cup (60 mL) vegetable oil
1 cup (115 g) grated Cheddar
cheese
8 ounces (240 g) cooked ham,
diced
2 tablespoons diced scallion

Opposite: Ham and Cheese Muffins

PEANUT BUTTER AND SUN S'MORES

SERVES 1

INGREDIENTS

1 graham cracker square,
broken in half
1 to 2 tablespoons peanut butter
⅓ (1.45-ounce/43-g) milk
chocolate bar
1 large marshmallow

There are a couple of ways to do s'mores: the hard way and the easy way. There's even a variation in between. But the easiest way is to let nature do it. Just wrap individual s'more packets tightly, so no bugs can get in, and leave them out in a warm spot for an hour or two. Hey, you've got perfectly melted chocolate and marshmallow. The hard way is to bring all the stuff to the site unassembled and try to roast the marshmallows over the fire, then stuff them between the crackers and the chocolate, thus ensuring that at least one s'more per person hits the dust and at least one person under eight gets second-degree marshmallow burns. Here again, the trick is to have them wrapped in foil so you can put them somewhere near the fire, not on it, and let nature do the melting.

For each s'more, spread one side of each graham cracker square lightly with peanut butter. Place chocolate on top of peanut butter, place marshmallow on top of chocolate and firmly press down the other graham cracker square, peanut butter side down.

Be firm: crush the marshmallow. But do so gently, so you don't smash the cracker in the process. Tightly wrap s'more with foil, using two thicknesses if you plan to heat it near the fire.

To serve, leave in a warm, shady spot for an hour or so, or carry, well-wrapped and with plenty of napkins, in a backpack close to your body.

To heat by a campfire, place on a warm rock near but not in the fire. Turn occasionally so heat distributes evenly and s'mores don't burn.

TAKE-ALONG HERO

SERVES 3 TO 4

INGREDIENTS

1 long loaf sourdough French
bread (approximately 12 inches/
30 cm long)
1 jar (6 ounces/180 g)
marinated artichoke hearts,
drained and coarsely chopped,
liquid reserved
½ cup (120 mL) mayonnaise
3 ounces (100 g) ham,
thinly sliced
3 ounces (100 g) salami or
summer sausage,
thinly sliced
3 ounces (100 g) turkey breast,
thinly sliced
3 ounces (100 g) Swiss cheese,
thinly sliced
⅓ cup (40 g) red onion,
thinly sliced
1 small can (3¼ ounces/100 g)
sliced ripe olives, drained
3 plum tomatoes, sliced

*This sandwich is great to make the
night before, ready to pack in a cooler
the next day. It needs some time for
the flavors to meld and to give it the
right texture to hold together, making
it easy to eat on the road or sitting
under a shade tree.*

*Cut bread in half horizontally.
Hollow out each half, leaving a ¾-
inch (2-cm) shell. Reserve scooped-out
bread for another use, if desired.*

*In small bowl, combine artichoke
liquid and mayonnaise. Spread
mixture onto each bread shell. In one
half of bread shell, layer meats,
turkey, cheese, artichokes, onion,
olives and tomatoes. Top with
remaining bread.*

*Wrap entire loaf tightly with plastic.
Overwrap tightly with aluminum foil
and refrigerate overnight. If
refrigerator space allows, place a
cookie sheet weighted with unopened
cans on top of sandwich to "set" it.*

*For easier serving, unwrap sandwich
and cut into 2-inch (5-cm) slices,*

*then rewrap securely, again in plastic
and foil. Place inside large plastic
bag and seal. Keep refrigerated or in
cooler until serving time.*

PRISSY'S CRUNCHING THROUGH THE SNOW WHITE CHOCOLATE CHIP COOKIES

MAKES 6 DOZEN

INGREDIENTS

½ cup (120 g) butter or margarine, softened
1 cup (180 g) firmly packed brown sugar
1 cup (225 g) granulated sugar
2 eggs
1 teaspoon vanilla
2 cups (225 g) all-purpose flour
1 teaspoon baking soda
½ teaspoon baking powder
¼ teaspoon salt
12 ounces (350 g) white chocolate, coarsely chopped
1 cup (115 g) pecans, coarsely chopped
2 cups (50 g) crispy rice cereal

A variation on the tried-and-true theme of chocolate chip cookies: These go crunch, which makes them great to eat while backpacking. As long as the leader is munching and crunching, the rest of the pack can't get lost if they're within earshot.

Preheat oven to 350°F (180°C). Cream butter and sugars until smooth, about 3 minutes. Add eggs and vanilla and beat until smooth and fluffy.

Mix flour, baking soda, baking powder and salt. Gradually blend dry ingredients into creamed mixture. Fold in white chocolate, nuts and cereal just until mixed.

Place 2-inch (5-cm) mounds of dough about 2 inches (5 cm) apart on ungreased cookie sheets. Bake for 10 to 12 minutes or until golden brown. Promptly transfer from baking sheets to wire racks to cool.

Variation

Substitute peanut butter or chocolate chips (or a combination) for white chocolate chips.

INSTANT GRATIFICATION

Sometimes the urge to snack is inhibited by lack of preparation time. These VERY fast and easy recipes solve that problem. Just make sure you've got the staples on hand and snacking need never require time, effort or a trip to the store.

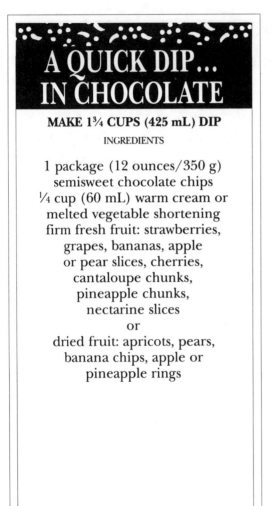

A QUICK DIP... IN CHOCOLATE

MAKE 1¾ CUPS (425 mL) DIP

INGREDIENTS

1 package (12 ounces/350 g)
semisweet chocolate chips
¼ cup (60 mL) warm cream or
melted vegetable shortening
firm fresh fruit: strawberries,
grapes, bananas, apple
or pear slices, cherries,
cantaloupe chunks,
pineapple chunks,
nectarine slices
or
dried fruit: apricots, pears,
banana chips, apple or
pineapple rings

Place chocolate chips in microwave-safe bowl and heat on high power until melted, about 1 minute. Stir. (Or place chocolate chips in top of double boiler over hot, not simmering, water and stir until melted.)

Stir in cream or shortening. Reheat if needed to maintain dipping consistency. Add another teaspoon or so of cream or shortening to thin if needed.

To serve, pass fruit and chocolate for dipping.

Variations

1. *Combine 6 ounces (180 g) each semisweet chocolate chips and peanut butter chips.*
2. *Use 1 package (12 ounces/350 g) white chocolate chips.*

Truly simple and easy, but decadent enough for the czars.

Reserve 4 pretty strawberries with stems for garnish. Combine yogurt or sour cream, vanilla and brown sugar. Stir until sugar is dissolved and sauce is smooth. Place a small portion of sauce in bottom of each of four small, clear bowls. Divide strawberries evenly and place in bowls. Top each with remaining sauce. Garnish, if desired, with whole berry and mint sprigs.

WORLD'S EASIEST STRAWBERRIES ROMANOFF

SERVES 4

INGREDIENTS

1 cup (240 mL) plain yogurt or
sour cream
1 teaspoon vanilla
3 to 4 tablespoons firmly packed
brown sugar
1 pint small strawberries,
stemmed, rinsed and dried
(halve strawberries if small
ones are not available)
mint sprigs, if available

BAKED BANANA SPLIT

SERVES 1

INGREDIENTS

1 banana
2 scoops vanilla (or other)
ice cream
2 tablespoons bottled
chocolate sauce
1 tablespoon chopped nuts
2 dollops of whipped cream
(optional)

This is a simply wonderful way to satisfy a craving for sweets. You can do it richly, in the tradition of the banana split, or with a low-calorie version. Any way you do it, it's a great way to eat a banana.

Preheat oven to 325°F (165°C). Place unpeeled banana on foil-lined baking sheet. Bake for 20 to 25 minutes or until peel is dark.

To serve, place banana on small plate or in banana split bowls. Slit open peel and place ice cream over banana. Top with chocolate sauce, nuts and whipped cream, if desired. Eat out of peel with spoon.

Variation

For a lower-calorie version, squeeze juice from 1 lemon or lime wedge over baked banana after slitting open peel. Top with 1 tablespoon honey or syrup.

OK, so you don't normally keep canned pie filling on hand, much less refrigerated. But this is different. Trust me, in a pinch, this is the closest you'll come to mousse in three minutes or less.

Empty pie filling into large bowl. Gently fold in whipped cream or topping and desired spirit for flavoring.

Spoon into serving dishes.

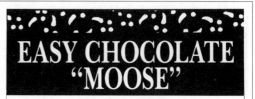

EASY CHOCOLATE "MOOSE"

SERVES 6 TO 8

INGREDIENTS

1 can (21 ounces/630 g)
chocolate pie filling, chilled
1 cup (240 mL) heavy cream,
whipped, or 1 carton
(8 ounces/240 g) non-dairy
whipped topping
3 tablespoons brandy, bourbon,
orange liqueur or kirsch

CHOCOLATE PEANUT BUTTER COOKIES

SERVES 1 TO 10

INGREDIENTS

1 package (any size) soft-style
peanut butter cookies
(may also use homemade;
see recipe on page 61)
1 package (any size)
ready-to-spread milk
chocolate frosting

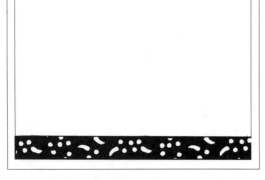

This is so simple it's almost cheating. But who cares? When the urge strikes, make satisfaction easy on yourself.

Spread cookies with frosting. Eat standing up to minimize calorie intake.

Serve with whole milk, or 2 percent if you insist on watching your butterfat. Skim milk takes the edge off this simple indulgence.

Nothing could be easier or seem more elaborate than Bourbon Street Apples and Ice Cream. It's just a matter of being prepared with the ingredients on hand.

Gently heat pie filling in saucepan over low heat or in microwave on medium-high power, stirring occasionally. Stir in bourbon to taste and cook briefly to dissipate alcohol. Spoon over ice cream in individual serving dishes.

BOURBON STREET APPLES AND ICE CREAM

SERVES 4 TO 6

INGREDIENTS

1 can (21 ounces/630 g) apple
pie filling
1 to 2 tablespoons bourbon,
or to taste
1 quart (1 L) pecan praline
or vanilla ice cream

A TRIFLE EASY

SERVES 6 TO 8

INGREDIENTS

1 package (4 ounces/120 g)
instant chocolate fudge
pudding mix
1 cup (240 mL) milk
1 carton (8 ounces/240 mL)
"light" or regular sour cream
1 cup (240 mL) heavy cream
¼ cup (60 g) sugar
1 teaspoon vanilla
2 cups (120 g) 1-inch/2.5-cm
chunks of angel food
or pound cake
(even 3 packages of
Twinkies will do)
¼ cup (60 mL) brandy
Shaved chocolate or berries
(optional)

This is as easy as trifle can get.

Prepare chocolate pudding according to package directions, using milk and sour cream.

Whip cream until frothy. Gradually add sugar and vanilla, beating until stiff.

Spoon a thin layer of chocolate pudding into clear dish with steep sides. Place ⅓ of the cake on top and sprinkle with ⅓ of the brandy. Spread ⅓ of the chocolate pudding over cake. Layer ⅓ of the whipped cream over the chocolate.

Repeat layers with ⅓ cake, ⅓ brandy, ⅓ chocolate pudding and ⅓ of the whipped cream.

Repeat layers again, using all remaining ingredients and ending with whipped cream. Decorate with shaved chocolate or fresh berries, if desired.

Eat it now if you must, but this tastes better after a few hours (8 is optimum) in the refrigerator.

HEALTH NUTS

Much food that is considered healthy is also boring, too chewy and not very good. These recipes don't fit that stereotype. While they're more health-conscious than some other indulgences in this book, they're still delightful; you won't know you're eating "health food" unless you're told.

GRILLED PEANUT BUTTER AND BANANA SANDWICH

SERVES 1

INGREDIENTS

2 slices wholewheat bread
2 to 3 tablespoons smooth or
crunchy peanut butter
½ banana, sliced
1 egg, lightly beaten
1 tablespoon butter or margarine
honey (optional)

This very American variation on the croque monsieur sandwich is definitely kids' stuff, but it is for the young at heart and palate as well as for children.

Spread one side of each slice of bread with peanut butter. Arrange slices of banana on peanut buttered side of one slice. Top with second slice, peanut butter side down.

Dip each side of sandwich in beaten egg, allow it to absorb as much egg as possible.

Melt butter in small skillet over medium-high heat and brown

Opposite: Fruit and Yogurt Dip (p.78)

For true snack-ability, these should be served as miniburgers—ideally, between fine whole-grain rolls.

Sauté scallion in olive oil until soft. Remove from heat. Combine scallion with tofu, rice, cheese, sesame seeds, flour, eggs and seasonings.

If time allows, chill mixture 20 minutes for easier handling. Shape into 2- to 3-inch (5- to 7-cm) patties. Fry in a skillet in a small amount of oil over medium heat until golden and crusty on each side.

Serve between warm rolls, garnished as desired with tomato, onion, alfalfa sprouts, mustard and mayonnaise.

To prepare in advance, place patties between buns and wrap tightly in foil. Keep warm in 200°F (95°C) oven for no longer than an hour.

GREAT LITTLE VEGGIE BURGERS

SERVES 8 TO 10

INGREDIENTS

2 tablespoons minced scallion, white part only
2 tablespoons olive oil
8 ounces (225 g) tofu, drained and mashed
1 cup (115 g) cooked brown rice
½ cup (60 g) grated low-fat mozzarella or Monterey Jack cheese
2 tablespoons toasted sesame seeds
⅓ cup (40 g) wholewheat flour
2 eggs, lightly beaten
1 teaspoon salt
1 tablespoon soy sauce
½ teaspoon dried basil
8 to 10 whole-grain rolls, split and warmed
Optional garnishes:
plum tomato slices
thin slices of red onion
alfalfa sprouts
mustard, mayonnaise

Opposite: Great Little Veggie Burgers

KYRA'S OAT BRAN CRUNCHIES

MAKES 48

INGREDIENTS

1 cup (225 g) margarine
2 cups (450 g) granulated or
brown sugar
3 tablespoons honey
2 teaspoons baking soda
2 cups (225 g) unbleached flour
3 cups (270 g) rolled oats
¾ cup (80 g) oat bran

A good friend, Kyra Effren, developed this recipe. I challenged her to come up with something delicious using oat bran—that miracle fiber that actually helps absorb cholesterol in the blood. Leave it to Kyra. These are good and good for you.

Preheat oven to 350°F (180°C). Grease a 10 x 15-inch (25 x 38-cm) cookie sheet or jellyroll pan.

Combine margarine, sugar, and honey in saucepan and bring to simmer. Add baking soda and allow to foam. Remove from heat.

Combine flour, oats, and oat bran in a large bowl. Pour in margarine mixture and mix until no more dry ingredients are visible.

Pile batter into prepared pan and press into an even layer. Bake for 15 to 20 minutes or until browned and slightly puffy.

Remove from oven; immediately cut into squares. Let cool in pan, then remove cookies and store in an airtight container.

These high-fiber muffins with bran and pineapple are good and chewy. Strict cholesterol watchers, be aware that the muffins contain eggs; you may want to use an egg substitute.

There's also a devil-may-care version of these muffins, certainly richer and tastier but with more saturated fat, since it contains coconut cream and a spread of coconut cream and butter. Delicious—but caveat emptor!

Preheat oven to 400°F (200°C). While oven is heating, spread bran flakes on a cookie sheet and place in oven just to crisp and brown, about 5 minutes; be careful not to burn.

Grease cups and top surface of a 9-cup pan.

Combine dry ingredients in medium bowl. Add oil, eggs and milk and mix just until blended. Fold in pineapple and vanilla; don't overmix. Spoon into prepared muffin tins, filling to the top.

Bake 15 to 20 minutes or until golden brown; do not overbake.

HAWAIIAN BRAN MUFFINS

MAKES 9 OVERSIZE MUFFINS

INGREDIENTS

1¼ cups (40 g) bran flakes
1¼ cups (150 g) unbleached flour
¼ cup (60 g) sugar
1 teaspoon baking powder
¼ teaspoon nutmeg
½ teaspoon salt
¼ cup (60 mL) vegetable oil
2 eggs, lightly beaten
¾ cup (180 mL) nonfat or lowfat milk or ½ cup (120 mL) cream of coconut
1 can (8 ounces/225 g) crushed pineapple, drained
½ teaspoon vanilla

Transfer to wire rack to cool. Serve warm or at room temperature.

For an occasional splurge, serve muffins warm with Coconut Butter: Cream ¼ cup (60 g) softened butter and 1 tablespoon cream of coconut. Return to refrigerator for 20 minutes

QUICK FIXES

This chapter is devoted to fast little meals or snacks, most of which come together in 30 minutes or less. Some require pre-preparation, but most can be done quickly, almost without thinking.

SOFT CORN TACOS

SERVES 4 TO 6

INGREDIENTS

12 soft corn tortillas
1 can (8 ounces/250 g) Mexican
corn, drained
Mexican rice (recipe follows)
1½ cups (175 g) grated low-fat
mozzarella, Monterey Jack or
Cheddar cheese
Salsa (optional)
about 2 cups (225 g) finely
shredded lettuce
about 1 cup (115 g) finely
chopped tomatoes
½ cup (60 g) chopped onions
(optional)
sliced jalapeños (optional)

These tacos can be a most fulfilling light meal on a hot summer day, with fruit for dessert, or just as rewarding on a cool fall day with a side dish of chili beans. This is definitely finger food, to be rolled tightly and eaten without inhibition.

Tightly wrap tortillas in foil and place in 300°F (150°C) oven for 20 minutes. Meanwhile, combine corn with rice and heat through. Have ready the cheese, rice mixture and garnishes.

To assemble, place even amounts of rice mixture and cheese in center of hot tortilla and fold in half. Place side by side, in shallow baking dish, approximately 9 x 6 inches (22 x 15 cm). Cover with foil and warm in 300°F (150°C) oven for 20 minutes, or for an hour at lowest oven temperature.

To serve, offer salsa, lettuce, tomatoes, onions and jalapeños alongside.

Heat oil in a saucepan over medium heat. Add rice and cook until opaque, stirring frequently. Add onion and cook until it is wilted and rice begins to brown. Add salt, water, tomato juice, cumin and chili powder and bring to boil. Reduce heat, cover and simmer until rice is tender and liquid is absorbed, 16 to 20 minutes. Remove lid, fluff rice and serve.

This can be made ahead and reheated. It goes well with grilled meats, fish or poultry.

MEXICAN RICE

SERVES 4 TO 6

INGREDIENTS

3 tablespoons olive or
vegetable oil
1 cup (150 g) raw rice
1 medium-size yellow onion,
chopped
½ teaspoon salt
1 cup (240 mL) warm water
1 cup (500 mL) tomato juice,
warmed
1 teaspoon ground cumin
1 tablespoon chili powder

CHICKEN BREAST SANDWICHES

SERVES 4

INGREDIENTS

4 boneless, skinless chicken
breast halves
salt and pepper to taste
1 tablespoon olive oil
4 thin slices Monterey Jack
cheese, regular or
with jalapeños
4 wholewheat hamburger buns,
heated or toasted if desired
mayonnaise and mustard
to taste
4 leaves of leaf lettuce
2 to 3 plum tomatoes, sliced

Such a quick and easy meal ought not to be so satisfying—but it is. Don't worry about marinating the breasts. A good dash of seasoning is all you need.

Gently pound chicken breast halves to flatten evenly. Season with salt and pepper. Heat olive oil in large skillet over medium-high heat. Sauté chicken breast halves until cooked through, about 3 to 4 minutes on each side.

Remove from heat and place a slice of cheese on each breast piece. Set aside to melt.

Split buns and spread mayonnaise and mustard on bottom halves. Place chicken breasts on buns and top with lettuce and tomatoes. Generously salt and pepper the tomatoes. Top with remaining bun.

Opposite: Hot Wings (p.15)

This is a great dish for informal entertaining or just down and dirty family eating. It's quick, easy and delicious.

Rinse and dry shrimp, leaving shells on. Melt butter in large skillet over low heat. When butter is melted add red pepper sauce and lemon juice. Increase heat to medium high.

Add shrimp and cook just until shrimp turn pink; do not overcook. Add salt to taste. Serve shrimp in bowls with plenty of butter, and ample amounts of bread for dipping into the butter.

Also provide plenty of napkins and newspaper in the middle of the table for discarding shells.

NEW ORLEANS SHRIMP

SERVES 4

INGREDIENTS

2 pounds (900 g) raw jumbo
(12 to 15 count) shrimp
1 cup (240 g) butter
¼ cup hot pepper sauce, or to taste
juice of 1 lemon
salt to taste
2 loaves crusty French bread

Opposite: New Orleans Shrimp

IN A STEW WITH PASTA

SERVES 4 TO 6

INGREDIENTS

2 cans (14½ ounces/435 g each)
chicken broth
1 can (14½ ounces/435 g) beef
broth
8 ounces (225 g) Italian sausage
1 package (12 to 16 ounces/350
to 450 g) frozen vegetables
for soup
8 ounces (225 g) fresh tortellini,
capelletti or other stuffed,
bite-size pasta
2 cups (500 mL) prepared
spaghetti sauce

This is one of the quickest stew recipes you'll ever encounter. Also one of the best. Serve it with garlic bread and a Caesar salad.

Empty broths into large stewpot and bring to boil. Meanwhile, crumble sausage into skillet and brown. Add vegetables to broth and allow liquid to return to boil. Reduce heat slightly and simmer for 10 minutes.

Drain grease from sausage. Add pasta and sausage to stewpot and cook pasta according to manufacturer's directions, about 7 to 8 minutes.

Stir in spaghetti sauce, gently blending well. Heat through and serve.

The best thing about this dish is the no-cook character of the sauce. So simple, so divine!

Bring large pot of salted water to boil. Add spaghetti and cook al dente, or just tender to the tooth, according to package directions.

Meanwhile, seed and chop tomatoes. Place olive oil in saucepan with shallots and garlic. Heat gently until oil is hot but not bubbly; swirls should be visible in the oil. Keep warm.

Toss together the tomatoes and olives.

When spaghetti is done, drain in a colander and place on heated serving platter or dish, preferably a large pasta dish. Place tomatoes on top of spaghetti, then pour hot oil over spaghetti and toss to coat strands evenly. Add salt to taste. Serve with plenty of fresh grated Parmesan cheese and red pepper, if desired.

SPAGHETTI WITH NO-COOK TOMATO SAUCE

SERVES 4

INGREDIENTS

8 ounces (225 g) spaghetti
6 to 8 plum tomatoes, seeded and chopped
½ cup (120 mL) olive oil
1 to 2 shallots, finely chopped
1 clove garlic, finely chopped
½ cup (60 g) chopped black olives or 1 cup (115 g) imported black olives, unseeded
salt to taste
freshly grated Parmesan cheese
dried red pepper, optional

FAST FAJITAS

SERVES 4

INGREDIENTS

12 flour tortillas
1 can (10 ounces/300 g) refried
beans, optional
2 teaspoons black pepper
2 teaspoons chili powder
½ teaspoon paprika
¼ teaspoon cayenne pepper
or to taste
½ teaspoon salt
1 pound (450 g) boneless,
skinless chicken breasts or beef
sirloin steak, well trimmed
2 tablespoons vegetable oil
1 onion, thinly sliced
1 green pepper, seeded and
thinly sliced
guacamole (see page 00),
if desired
bottled salsa

Fajitas, whether chicken or beef, don't have to be marinated to be juicy and tender. Some seasoning adjustments are required to make this quick version, but when hunger strikes, time isn't on your side.

Preheat oven to 300°F (150°C). Wrap tortilla tightly in foil and place in oven for 20 minutes or until heated through. Keep warm. Place refried beans in saucepan and gently heat through. Keep warm.

Meanwhile, combine black pepper, chili powder, paprika, cayenne pepper and salt on plate or waxed paper. Cut chicken or beef into strips about 2 inches (5 cm) long and ½ inch (1 cm) wide. Press strips into seasoning mixture to evenly coat all sides.

Heat oil over medium-high heat in large skillet. Add chicken or beef, shaking off excess seasoning, and sauté over high heat until cooked through. Remove from skillet and keep warm.

Over high heat, sauté onion and green pepper strips, adding more oil if

*necessary. Remove from skillet and
keep warm.*

*Have each diner assemble his own
fajitas: Spread warm tortilla with
refried beans, then with guacamole.
Place chicken or beef in the center,
along with salsa, if desired. Roll up
and eat.*

EYE OPENER

SERVES 1

INGREDIENTS

1 sandwich slice low-fat ham or chicken
1 canned pineapple ring or sliced fresh apple ring
1 thin slice low-fat mozzarella cheese
1 teaspoon vinegar
1 egg
salt and pepper
salsa or hot pepper sauce (optional)

This low-fat breakfast-style snack will get you up and out when you need to be alert and ready for business or pleasure. It's designed to be high in protein and low in fat for maximum performance.

Place ham or chicken slice on microwave-safe plate. Top with pineapple or apple ring and cheese.

Bring water to boil in small saucepan for poaching egg. When water simmers, add vinegar.

Whirl water and slide egg into whirlpool. Poach 3 to 5 minutes, depending on how firm you prefer your eggs. When egg is done, remove from water with slotted spoon. Place spoon on paper towel to absorb water.

Meanwhile, microwave ham stack for 1 minute on high power. Top with poached egg. Season to taste with salt and pepper. Add salsa or hot pepper sauce, if desired.

COMFORT FOOD

"Mommy food" is another way to describe these dishes. Whether Mom actually made them doesn't matter, but we wish she had. Classic heartwarmers, these recipes range from homey bread pudding to baked apples and a sublime kugel.

FEEL BETTER BREAD PUDDING

SERVES 6 TO 8

INGREDIENTS

3 cups (180 g) finely diced
day-old bread
(crusts removed)
½ cup (60 g) golden raisins
1 can (14 ounces/420 g)
sweetened condensed
milk
3 cups (720 mL) very hot water
3 eggs, lightly beaten
¼ teaspoon cinnamon
⅛ teaspoon nutmeg
1 tablespoon melted butter
½ teaspoon salt
1 teaspoon vanilla or 2
tablespoons bourbon
whipped cream or chocolate
sauce (optional)

Nothing is any more comfortingly gooey than bread pudding made in the New Orleans tradition. Whether home is the Deep South or "up nawth," bread pudding can do away with the blues.

Butter a 1½-quart (1.5-L) baking dish. Place diced bread and raisins in baking dish. Toss to distribute raisins evenly throughout.

Combine condensed milk and water. Pour over bread and let stand until lukewarm.

Meanwhile, combine eggs, cinnamon, nutmeg, butter, salt and vanilla or bourbon.

Pour over bread in casserole. Let stand about 20 minutes. Meanwhile, preheat oven to 350°F (180°C). Set baking dish in shallow pan of hot water. Bake uncovered about 1 hour or until knife inserted in center comes out clean.

If desired, serve with whipped cream or chocolate sauce.

Opposite: Feel Better Bread Pudding

This is one of the oldest cake recipes around; just about every region claims it. It is standard "Mommy food" wherever you go.

Preheat oven to 400°F (200°C). Grease 15½ x 10½-inch (39 x 25-cm) jellyroll pan. Sift together sugar and flour in large bowl. Combine margarine, shortening, cocoa and water in saucepan and bring to rapid boil. Pour over dry ingredients and stir well. Add buttermilk, eggs, baking soda and vanilla and mix well.

Pour batter into prepared pan and bake 20 minutes.

Five minutes before cake is done, prepare icing: Combine margarine, cocoa and milk in saucepan and cook over low heat until margarine is melted, then bring to a boil. Remove from heat. Add powdered sugar, vanilla and pecans and beat well. Spread over hot cake as soon as it comes out of the oven, while it is still in the pan.

CHOCOLATE SHEET CAKE

MAKES 15 3-INCH (7.5-CM) SQUARES

INGREDIENTS

2 cups (450 g) sugar
2 cups (225 g) all-purpose flour
½ cup (120 g) margarine
½ cup (120 g) shortening
¼ cup (30 g) cocoa
1 cup (240 mL) water
½ cup (120 mL) buttermilk
2 eggs, lightly beaten
1 teaspoon baking soda
1 teaspoon vanilla

ICING

½ cup (120 g) margarine
¼ cup (30 g) cocoa
⅓ cup (80 mL) milk
1 pound (450 g) powdered sugar
1 teaspoon vanilla
1 cup (115 g) chopped pecans

Opposite: Peanut Butter Cookies (p.61)

MOMMY'S BAKED CUSTARD

SERVES 12

INGREDIENTS

5 large eggs
¾ cup (180 g) sugar
¼ teaspoon salt
1 teaspoon vanilla
4 cups (1 quart/1 L) milk,
scalded
nutmeg

No chapter on comfort food would be complete without custard. The only question is, baked or stirred? Well, I'm coming down on the side of baked. There's just something about the little ovenproof glass custard cups that says comfort and "Mommy loves you." The worst thing about making custard is getting the cups and the hot water bath ready, so do that first while you're really in the mood.

Place 12 custard cups in a shallow baking pan. Begin heating enough water to pour into pan to a depth of 1 inch (2.5 cm). Preheat oven to 325°F (165°C).

Beat eggs lightly with sugar, salt and vanilla. Gradually, stir in hot milk. For easier handling, transfer custard to large measuring cup or pitcher with pouring spout. Pour into custard cups and sprinkle with nutmeg. Place in oven.

Carefully pour hot water into baking pan to depth of 1 inch (2.5 cm). Close oven door and bake about 1¼ hours or until a knife inserted midway between center and rim of

custard comes out clean.

Remove custards from water bath and cool to room temperature. Chill before serving, if desired.

VERY FLUFFY TAPIOCA

SERVES 4

INGREDIENTS

3 tablespoons quick-cooking
tapioca
⅛ teaspoon salt
5 tablespoons sugar
2 cups (500 mL) milk
2 eggs, separated
¾ teaspoon vanilla

This is the homiest of all Mommy-foods for me. When the going gets tough, I get tapioca.

Combine tapioca, salt, 3 tablespoons sugar, milk and egg yolks in saucepan and let stand 5 minutes.

Meanwhile, beat egg whites until foamy. Gradually add 2 tablespoons sugar, beating to soft peaks. Set aside.

Cook tapioca mixture over medium heat to a full boil, stirring constantly. Remove from heat when mixture begins to thicken.

Gradually add to beaten white, stirring quickly just until blended. Stir in vanilla. Cool 20 minutes. Stir.

These cookies are a dough-lover's dream come true. If there's enough dough left to make the cookies, these are the kind you wish Mom had made. My kids pronounced them "as good as the soft ones at the store"—I took it as a compliment.

Cookies and milk—nothing could be more comforting. If things are really tough, make sure you've got a pint of chocolate milk on hand for the classic flavor combo of chocolate and peanut butter.

Cream together shortening or butter and sugars until light and fluffy. Beat in eggs and vanilla, then peanut butter.

In separate bowl, sift together flour, salt and baking powder. Mix dry ingredients into peanut butter mixture about $1/3$ at a time. For easier handling, chill dough about 1 hour.

Preheat oven to 375°F (190°C). Grease cookie sheets. For easier handling, chill dough about 1 hour. Roll dough into 1-inch (2.5-cm) balls. Arrange about 2 inches (5 cm) apart on prepared cookie sheets.

PEANUT BUTTER COOKIES

MAKES 5 TO 6 DOZEN

INGREDIENTS

1 cup (225 g) shortening or butter or
equal amounts of both
1 cup (225 g) granulated sugar
1 cup (225 g) firmly packed light brown sugar
2 eggs
1 teaspoon vanilla
1 cup (225 g) peanut butter, smooth or crunchy (preferably natural, unsweetened)
$2\frac{1}{2}$ cups (300 g) all-purpose flour
$\frac{1}{2}$ teaspoon salt
1 teaspoon baking powder

*Flatten by pressing lightly with a
floured fork in a crisscross pattern.
Bake for 10 to 12 minutes or until
golden.*

*Cook 10 minutes on cookie sheets,
then transfer to wire rack.*

Variation

*Frost each cookie with prepared milk
chocolate frosting.*

Variation

*Before baking, make a thumbprint
indentation and fill center of each
cookie with ½ teaspoon grape jelly.*

Pour cold milk or cream over hot cobbler and you've got a dish you imagine your grandmother in the country had made.

Preheat oven to 375°F (190°C). Gently toss peaches with sugar, brandy and lemon juice (if omitting brandy increase lemon juice to 1 tablespoon). Sprinkle peaches with 3 tablespoons flour and gently toss again.

Spread peach mixture in a generously buttered 8-inch (20-cm) square pan.

In food processor or blender, grind ½ cup (60 g) pecans until fine; transfer to bowl. Add oats, brown sugar, ¼ cup (30 g) flour and cinnamon. Use a pastry blender, or pulse motion on food processor, to cut butter into rolled oat mixture. Do not over-process; mixture should be crumbly. Add remaining ½ cup (60 g) chopped pecans. Sprinkle nut topping over peaches.

Bake about 25 minutes or until peaches are tender and topping is golden brown; bake an additional 5 minutes if using frozen peaches.

COUNTRY PEACH CRISP

SERVES 6

INGREDIENTS

3 cups (350 g) sliced fresh or dry-pack frozen peaches
(2 to 3 large)
⅓ cup (75 g) granulated sugar
¼ cup (60 mL) brandy
(optional)
1 teaspoon fresh lemon juice
3 tablespoons all-purpose flour
1 cup (115 g) chopped pecans
½ cup (60 g) rolled oats
¼ cup (60 g) firmly packed brown sugar
¼ cup (30 g) all-purpose flour
1 teaspoon cinnamon
⅓ cup (80 g) butter, softened
cream or ice cream

Serve warm with cream or ice cream.
If necessary, reheat gently before
serving.

Opposite: Country Peach Crisp

Few things are more soothing than a dish of sweet noodle kugel. A Jewish tradition, it is as comforting to hurt feelings as chicken soup is to stuffy noses.

Cook noodles according to package directions. Drain and set aside.

Preheat oven to 375°F (190°C). Butter 9 x 13-inch (23 x 33-cm) baking dish. Arrange noodles in baking dish. Beat together eggs, sugar, salt, cinnamon, milk, butter and sour cream. Stir in raisins. Pour over noodles. Sprinkle with nutmeg.

Bake for 30 to 40 minutes or until set. Serve warm or at room temperature.

NOODLE KUGEL

SERVES 8
INGREDIENTS

1 package (12 ounces/350 g) fine egg noodles
4 eggs, well beaten
½ cup (115 g) sugar
1 teaspoon salt
1 teaspoon cinnamon
2 cups (500 mL) milk
½ cup (120 g) butter, melted
1 cup (240 mL) sour cream
½ cup (60 g) raisins
nutmeg

Opposite: Pecan Banana Scones (p.22)

BAKED APPLES

SERVES 4

INGREDIENTS

4 large cooking apples
½ cup (120 g) granulated sugar
combined with ½ teaspoon
cinnamon
4 tablespoons (30 g) golden
raisins
4 tablespoons (60 g) butter
½ cup (120 mL) water
4 tablespoons (60 g) firmly
packed brown sugar,
or to taste
ice cream, whipped cream or
heavy cream

This is one of my favorites from childhood. Warm, with cream, lots of sugar, cinnamon and raisins, baked apples were a special treat.

Preheat oven to 350°F (180°C). Core apples and peel about ⅓ of the way down; be careful not to pierce the bottom of the apple. Make a hole in top of each apple about 1 to 1½ inches (2.5 to 3.5 cm) in diameter. Place apples in ungreased shallow baking dish.

Spoon 2 tablespoons sugar-cinnamon mixture into hollow of each apple. Fill with 1 tablespoon raisins and top with 1 tablespoon butter. Press butter and raisins firmly into apple.

Pour water around apples and bake 45 minutes to 1 hour or until tender. When apples are done, remove from oven and sprinkle each with 1 tablespoon brown sugar. Broil 4 inches from heat for about 1 to 2 minutes or until sugar bubbles.

Serve warm or cold with ice cream, whipped cream or heavy cream.

When insomnia strikes, and I'm talking serious stuff, don't just lie there. Get up and make this rice pudding. Read while it bakes and cools slightly. Eat a bowl and go to sleep. It's a better way to kill an hour of sleeplessness than tossing and turning.

Combine rice, milk, sugar and butter in top of double boiler over direct heat and bring just to boil. Meanwhile, bring water to boil in bottom of double boiler.

When milk mixture boils, place over boiling water and cook, covered, stirring occasionally, for about 20 minutes or until rice is tender but not fully cooked. Remove from heat.

Beat eggs and vanilla in medium bowl. Slowly add small portion of hot rice mixture to eggs, then slowly whisk eggs back into rice mixture.

Preheat oven to 350°F (180°C). Transfer pudding to a buttered rectangular 1½-quart (1.5 L) casserole and bake 20 minutes. Remove pudding from oven and mix well. Sprinkle top with nutmeg or

RICE PUDDING

SERVES 8 TO 10

INGREDIENTS

½ cup (90 g) raw rice (medium- or short-grain works better than converted or long-grain)
4 cups (1 quart/1 L) milk
½ cup plus 2 tablespoons (150 g) sugar
3 tablespoons butter
3 eggs beaten
1½ teaspoons vanilla
nutmeg or cinnamon

*cinnamon and return to oven for
another 20 minutes.*

Microwave Method

*Combine rice, milk, sugar and butter
in microwave-safe 2-quart (2-L)
bowl. Cook on high power for 6
minutes. Stir, then cover with plastic
wrap and cook for 6 more minutes,
stirring again. Cook until rice is
tender but not fully cooked, about 3
to 5 minutes. Proceed as above,
beginning with beating eggs and
vanilla together. Finish in
conventional oven.*

ROAD FOOD

These recipes are made to be eaten while driving or riding in the car. Since the automobile plays such a dominant role in most people's lives, it's hard to overlook what is often the necessity of eating while on the road. If you can't munch in your own automobile, where can you munch?

BLACK-TOP BROWNIES

MAKES 9 3-INCH BROWNIES

INGREDIENTS

1¼ cups (225 g) semisweet
chocolate chips
½ cup (120 g) butter or
margarine, softened
1 cup (225 g) sugar
3 eggs
1 teaspoon vanilla
1 cup (120 g) all-purpose flour
½ teaspoon baking powder
¼ teaspoon salt
1 cup (115 g) chopped pecans

Of course, brownies could go in the chapter on comfort food, on sinful indulgences or In the Great Outdoors, but they had to go somewhere and I found them to be most at home for me in the car.

They aren't quite as messy as some other fun foods, and, let's face it, a long car trip should have its reward. Besides, brownies don't require utensils, just fingers and a napkin.

Lightly butter the bottom and sides of a 9-inch (23-cm) square baking pan. Preheat oven to 350°F (180°C). Melt ¾ cup (135 g) chocolate chips in top of double boiler over simmering water, or place chips in microwave-safe bowl and melt on high power for 1 minute. Stir to finish melting and set aside.

Cream butter and sugar in mixing bowl at high speed of electric mixer until light and fluffy. Add eggs one at a time and blend well. Beat in vanilla and chocolate.

Sift together flour, baking powder and salt. Blend dry ingredients into egg mixture, scraping down sides of

*bowl. Fold in nuts and remaining ¹/₂
cup (90 g) chocolate chips.*

*Spread batter in prepared pan and
bake for 25 to 30 minutes or just
until brownies begin to pull away
from sides of pan.*

Variation

*Use ¹/₂ cup (90 g) peanut butter chips
instead of ¹/₂ cup chocolate chips in
batter. Decrease chocolate chips to ³/₄
cup (135 g).*

CHIVES AND CHEESE TO GO

SERVES 6 TO 8

INGREDIENTS

6 to 8 flour tortillas
1 container (6 to 8 ounces/180
to 240 g) cream cheese
and chive spread
6 to 8 thin slices ham (optional)
salsa for dipping (optional)

This can be party food, but it adapts so well to munching in the car because it is bite-size and not too messy. Of course, dipping it in salsa can mean a dribble or two, but who cares?

Spread tortillas evenly with cream cheese. Place slice of ham on each if desired. Roll up tightly and fasten with toothpicks. Refrigerate several hours or overnight, tightly wrapped or in plastic bag.

Cut into 1-inch (2.5-cm) slices. Keep refrigerated and tightly wrapped until ready to serve. Serve with salsa for dipping, if desired.

Opposite: Black Top Brownies (p.70)

These are good for nibbling while you're driving along. Better have a soft drink close at hand, though, if you like things hot.

Preheat oven to 300°F (150°C). Combine oil and butter in large, shallow baking pan and place in oven until butter melts. Remove from oven and stir in brown sugar, breaking up any lumps, with pepper and salt. Mix well.

Add nuts and toss to coat evenly. Spread nuts in a single layer and bake for 20 minutes, stirring occasionally. Let cool before serving.

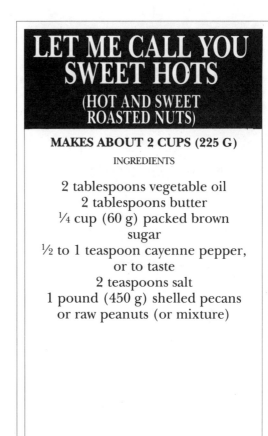

LET ME CALL YOU SWEET HOTS
(HOT AND SWEET ROASTED NUTS)

MAKES ABOUT 2 CUPS (225 G)

INGREDIENTS

2 tablespoons vegetable oil
2 tablespoons butter
¼ cup (60 g) packed brown sugar
½ to 1 teaspoon cayenne pepper, or to taste
2 teaspoons salt
1 pound (450 g) shelled pecans or raw peanuts (or mixture)

Opposite: Crispers (p.76)

"YOU'LL LOVE THIS LEMON" SQUARES

MAKES ABOUT 25

INGREDIENTS

1 cup (120 g) all-purpose flour
¼ cup (45 g) powdered sugar
½ cup (120 g) butter or
margarine, softened
1 cup (225 g) granulated sugar
2 eggs
2 tablespoons fresh lemon juice
2 teaspoons grated lemon peel
½ teaspoon salt
½ teaspoon baking powder

If you've ever gotten stuck with a lemon, you know that driving can be a drag. But these bar cookies are great—guaranteed to work every time.

Preheat oven to 350°F (180°C). Place flour and powdered sugar in small bowl and cut in butter until well mixed and crumbly. Press onto bottom and about ¾ inch (2-cm) up sides of ungreased 8-inch (20-cm) square baking pan. Bake 20 minutes. Remove from oven.

Beat together granulated sugar, eggs, lemon juice, lemon peel and salt. Stir in baking powder, mixing quickly but thoroughly. Pour over hot crust and return to oven for 25 minutes or until center is barely set (check after 15 minutes to see if top is getting too brown; if it is, place a piece of foil loosely over the top to slow browning).

Let cool, then cut into 1½-inch (4-cm) squares.

AFTER-SCHOOL SNACKS

Most of these recipes are easy enough for kids to make themselves, depending on their age and experience in the kitchen. Ages are provided for guidelines, but parents should study the recipes and keep their children's abilities in mind before letting them proceed solo. And, of course, youthful cooks should always get a parent's permission before starting a kitchen project, and must remember that cleaning up is part of the job.

CRISPERS

MAKES 2 DOZEN

INGREDIENTS

½ cup (120 g) butter or
margarine
1 package (10½ ounces/315 g)
miniature marshmallows,
plain or colored
5 cups (120 g) crispy rice cereal
1 package (6 ounces/180 g)
chocolate or peanut butter
chips*, or ¾ cup (120 g)
raisins or peanuts

*If desired, freeze chocolate or peanut
butter chips so they don't melt when
mixed with hot ingredients.

This recipe is recommended for
children 10 or older to make alone.
Younger children will need some
adult supervision.

Lightly coat 8-inch (20-cm) square
pan with nonstick spray.

Melt butter in large saucepan over
low heat, or in large glass measuring
cup or 2-quart (2-L) mixing bowl in
microwave on high power for 1 to 1½
minutes.

Add marshmallows and cook and stir
until melted, about 5 minutes over
direct heat or about 2 minutes on
high power in microwave. Stir until
mixture is smooth.

Combine cereal and other desired
ingredient(s). Add marshmallow
mixture and, working quickly, stir to
combine ingredients evenly. Spread
in prepared pan, press into an even
layer and let cool.

Cut into 2 dozen squares.

Really young ones may require adult assistance to slice the doughnuts and to measure and mix ingredients for this simple snack. But after that, it's a cinch for kids of most any age.

Halve doughnuts horizontally. Stir together peanut butter and honey to make a soft spread. Spread mixture on each doughnut half. If desired, place in toaster oven just long enough to heat peanut butter, or warm in preheated 350°F (180°C) oven for about 5 minutes.

PEANUTTY DOUGHNUTS

SERVES 2 TO 4

INGREDIENTS

2 cake doughnuts*
¼ cup (60 g) chunky peanut butter
2 tablespoons honey

*If desired, substitute bagels.

FRUIT
AND YOGURT
DIP

SERVES 1

INGREDIENTS

½ cup (120 mL) plain or vanilla
yogurt or sour cream
½ teaspoon vanilla (omit if using
vanilla yogurt)
1 to 2 tablespoons firmly packed
brown sugar, or to taste
approximately 1 cup (115 g)
seedless red or green grapes;
strawberries; pineapple, banana
or canteloupe chunks; and/or
apple, nectarine or pear slices.

This recipe may be in the kids' chapter, but don't let it fool you. It can taste a lot like the world's easiest Strawberries Romanoff. Check out the grownup variation in the chapter on Instant Gratification. Mix this up in advance, so all the kids have to do is dip and eat.

Combine yogurt, vanilla if desired, and brown sugar. Rinse and dry fruit. Using toothpicks or fingers, dip into yogurt.

Kids love microwave popcorn. This is a nice touch for plain popcorn, and simple enough for cooks 10 and older, if they can handle an oven.

Preheat oven to 350°F (180°C). Pop microwave popcorn according to manufacturer's directions. Carefully open package and pour into a large mixing bowl. Add pecans and toss to combine.

Meanwhile, combine butter and honey in a small saucepan and melt over low heat, stirring constantly, or place in glass measuring cup and heat in microwave on high power for 30 to 45 seconds. Stir to combine.

Pour honey mixture over popcorn and stir well to coat evenly. Spread popcorn on a nonstick baking sheet and bake for 8 to 10 minutes or until crisp; be careful not to burn. Let cool enough to handle and serve.

Variation

Use packaged prepopped popcorn, if desired, and omit popping step. This produces a salty snack, however, since packaged popcorn is seasoned.

POPCORN WITH HONEY AND NUTS

MAKE ABOUT 2 QUARTS

INGREDIENTS

1 package unsalted microwave popcorn (about 8 cups/2 L popped corn)
¾ cup (90 g) chopped pecans
¼ cup (60 g) butter or margarine
¼ cup (60 g) honey

BANANA CHILLERS

SERVES 1

INGREDIENTS

4 chunks (2-inch/5-cm) frozen
banana (approximately
1 banana)
½ cup (120 mL) milk
¼ teaspoon vanilla
1 tablespoon sugar (optional)
½ cup (120 mL) strawberry soda

This is a great way to use up ripe bananas. When the skins get blotchy or too dark for eating out of hand, cut bananas into 2-inch (5-cm) chunks and toss in the freezer. To tackle this alone, children should be old enough, usually about ten, to handle powerful equipment like a blender or food processor.

Combine banana chunks, milk, vanilla and sugar in food processor or blender and blend until smooth. Pour into glass, add strawberry soda and stir quickly. Serve immediately. This doubles easily to serve 2.

Kids can get pretty sick of sandwiches. These Ham Rolls, with crackers or breadsticks, are great after-school snacks or lunchbox stuffers. Children six and older can handle this one.

Combine jam and mustard to taste in a small bowl. Spread evenly on ham. Roll up each slice and fasten with a toothpick.

Serve with sweet pickles, if desired.

This is a variation on the Ham Roll theme, but with a little more substance. Children over six should be able to prepare these.

Layer 1 turkey slice and 1 cheese slice together; repeat with remainder to form 4 rolls. Place pickle spears in middle and roll turkey and cheese around it. Fasten with toothpicks.

Serve with crackers, if desired.

HAM ROLLS

SERVES 2

INGREDIENTS

2 tablespoons thick, chunky
strawberry or apricot jam
½ to 1 teaspoon Dijon or yellow
mustard
4 sandwich slices cooked ham
sweet pickles (optional)

TURKEY ROLLS

SERVES 2

INGREDIENTS

4 sandwich slices cooked turkey
or chicken
4 individual slices packaged Swiss
or American process cheese
4 kosher pickle spears, drained
on paper towel
assorted crackers (optional)

BANANA DIPPERS

SERVES 1

INGREDIENTS

1 banana, peeled and cut into
small chunks
a variety of dips in small bowls or
paper cups: honey, cinnamon
sugar, grated carrots, chocolate
syrup, maple syrup, applesauce,
flavored yogurt

Dipping is one of little kids' favorite ways to eat. It uses their God-given utensils, fingers, and excuses the inevitable mess. This also gives them a chance to experiment with tastes. For very young ones, don't give too many tastes at once; it'll simply bewilder them.

Peel banana and cut into pieces small enough for a young child to hold and fit into his mouth. Place desired dips in small shallow bowls or cups so the young gastronome can test the palatability of the offerings.

SWEET MOMENTS

*These sinful indulgences are supposed to make you feel guilty,
they're so good.*

HOT CHOCOLATE PUDDING CAKE

SERVES 6

INGREDIENTS

1 cup (120 g) all-purpose flour
2 teaspoons baking powder
¼ teaspoon salt
¾ cup (180 g) granulated sugar
½ cup (60 g) cocoa
½ cup (120 mL) milk
1 teaspoon vanilla
2 tablespoons vegetable oil
½ cup (60 g) coarsely
chopped nuts
1 cup (225 g) firmly packed
brown sugar
¼ teaspoon cinnamon or instant
coffee granules
1½ cups (360 mL) hot water

Winter or summer, this dessert fits the bill for chocolate lovers. In winter, serve it with whipped cream. In summer, add some ice cream— cinnamon is particularly nice—to cool things off.

Preheat oven to 350°F (180°C). Sift together flour, baking powder, salt, sugar and ¼ cup (30 g) cocoa. Add milk, vanilla and oil; stir well. Sprinkle in nuts. Spread in 1½-quart (1.5 L) casserole. Carefully combine brown sugar, cinnamon, remaining cocoa and hot water. Pour over mixture. Bake for 25 to 30 minutes or until top is cakelike and pudding bubbles through top.

This is the kind of apple pie you dream of at night or when you see the first shipment of crisp apples in the fall.

Preheat oven to 375°F (190°C). Combine 1 cup (225 g) sugar and 2 tablespoons flour. Add egg, sour cream, vanilla and salt and beat until sugar is dissolved. Fold in apples and raisins; pour into pie shell.

Combine remaining ½ cup (115 g) sugar and 5 tablespoons flour with butter and blend until crumbly. Sprinkle over top of pie.

Place cookie sheet on bottom oven rack to catch any drips. Loosely cover crust of pie with circle of aluminum foil. Place pie on center rack of oven. Bake for 45 minutes. Remove foil from crust and continue baking for 30 minutes longer. Let pie cool before cutting.

SOUR CREAM APPLE PIE

SERVES 8

INGREDIENTS

1½ cups (340 g) sugar
7 tablespoons all-purpose flour
1 egg, lightly beaten
1 cup (240 mL) sour cream
1½ teaspoons vanilla
¼ teaspoon salt
4 to 4½ cups (450 to 500 g)
peeled, cored and sliced
tart apples
(Granny Smith
or winesap)
½ cup (60 g) golden
or dark raisins
¼ cup (60 g) butter
or margarine
1 9-inch (22-cm) unbaked
deep-dish pie shell

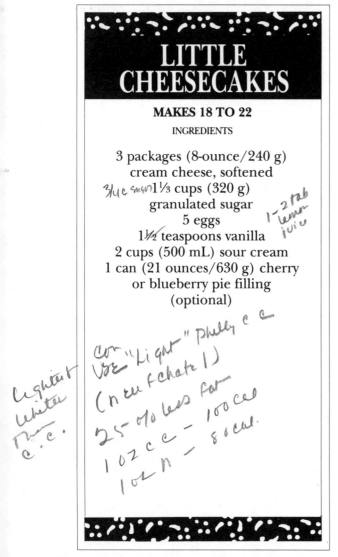

LITTLE CHEESECAKES

MAKES 18 TO 22

INGREDIENTS

3 packages (8-ounce/240 g)
cream cheese, softened
1 1/3 cups (320 g)
granulated sugar
5 eggs
1 1/2 teaspoons vanilla
2 cups (500 mL) sour cream
1 can (21 ounces/630 g) cherry
or blueberry pie filling
(optional)

(handwritten annotations) 3/4 c sugar · 1-2 tab lemon juice · Lightest whitest c.c. · or use "Light" philly c.c. (neufchatel) 25% less fat · 1 oz c c — 100 cal · 1 oz N — 80 cal.

These are great for snacking because you can make a bunch and freeze them. Thaw only as many as you will allow yourself at one time, knowing that you'll eat as many as are available at the earliest opportunity.

Preheat oven to 350°F (180°C). Cream together cream cheese and 1 cup (240 g) sugar until fluffy. Beat in eggs one at a time, then blend in 1 teaspoon vanilla. Line 18 muffin cups with paper liners and fill 2/3 full with cream cheese mixture.

Bake for 35 minutes. Remove from oven and let rest about 5 minutes, until tops sink.

Meanwhile, combine sour cream, 1/3 cup (80 g) sugar and 1/2 teaspoon vanilla. Spread each cheesecake with sour cream mixture and return to oven for 5 minutes. Let cool.

If desired, spread pie filling on each cheesecake before serving.

Tip

Cheesecakes can be frozen in muffin pans before spreading with pie *filling. When frozen, remove from pans and store in airtight plastic bags. Spread with pie filling after cheesecakes are thawed, just before serving.*

HOT FUDGE SUNDAE

SERVES 1

INGREDIENTS

2 to 3 scoops vanilla or other ice cream
¼ to ⅓ cup (60 to 80 mL) warm Homemade Chocolate Sauce (recipe follows)
1 to 2 tablespoons marshmallow creme
1 to 2 dollops whipped cream
1 to 2 tablespoons toasted slivered almonds
1 maraschino cherry, with stem (optional)

Sometimes a big sundae is just what you need. Go ahead—indulge. Forget about dinner. Just go for the hot, gooey chocolate, the smooth, white marshmallow creme, the chopped nuts, the frosty cold ice cream. I've always been partial to vanilla, but it's your sundae, so pick your flavor.

Place scoops of ice cream in bowl and return to freezer to harden. Prepare Homemade Chocolate Sauce and keep warm.

Remove ice cream from freezer and top with marshmallow creme, then warm chocolate sauce. Dollop with whipped cream, sprinkle with nuts and garnish with cherry.

Homemade Chocolate Sauce: Bring 1 cup (240 mL) heavy cream just to boil in heavy saucepan. Remove from heat and stir in 1⅓ cups (240 g) semisweet chocolate chips or 8 ounces (240 g) semisweet chocolate, coarsely chopped. Stir gently until sauce is smooth. Add 1 teaspoon vanilla.

Sauce may be made several days ahead, refrigerated and gently reheated.

It's impossible to eat a lot of this rich yet oh-so-easy dessert. But don't let that stop you from giving it a try. Spoon it into pot de crème dishes or pile it into small wine glasses for a dressier dessert. Top with unsweetened whipped cream and chopped nuts.

Preheat oven to 425°F (215°C). Pour sweetened condensed milk into a pie plate and cover loosely with foil. Bake for 1 hour or until golden and caramelized. Pour into four individual serving dishes. Cool and chill, if desired.

Serve with a dollop of unsweetened whipped cream and a sprinkling of nuts.

CARAMEL PUDDING

SERVES 4

INGREDIENTS

1 can (14 ounces/420 g) sweetened condensed milk
½ cup (120 mL) heavy cream, whipped
chopped nuts

Opposite: Peanutty Doughnuts (p.77)
Overleaf: Hot Fudge Sundae

CHOCOLATE TEMPTATION TOFFEE

MAKES 2 TO 2½ POUNDS
(900 TO 1125 G)

INGREDIENTS

3½ cups (420 g) pecan halves
1 cup (225 g) butter (do not use margarine)
5 tablespoons water
1 cup (225 g) sugar
1½ cups (270 g) milk chocolate chips

This toffee is so rich that even the most dedicated candy muncher will have to take a break. Don't be afraid that you can't overindulge. You can.

This also makes great gifts for many occasions. Give in airtight tins, the way it should be stored.

Reserve ½ cup (60 g) pecans and grind or chop medium fine.

Rub a 2-foot (60-cm) length of foil with butter. Arrange pecan halves in a single layer on the buttered foil.

Combine butter, water and sugar in heavy saucepan. Boil over medium-high heat until mixture reaches hard-crack stage (300 to 310°F/150 to 154°C) on candy thermometer, or until a drop of the mixture dropped into cold water forms brittle strands.

Quickly pour toffee mixture evenly over pecans. Sprinkle chocolate chips evenly over hot toffee mixture. Spread chocolate chips with spatula, if desired. Sprinkle with ground pecans.

Let cool to room temperature. Break into pieces. Store in airtight tins.

MUNCHER'S PANTRY

These are some of the devoted muncher's kitchen staples for Instant Gratification. Keep them on hand and you'll never be without something to snack on.

vanilla ice cream
pecan praline ice cream
apple pie filling
chocolate pie filling
chocolate chips
cream
plain yogurt
milk
"light" sour cream
fresh seasonal fruit
dried fruit
bananas
prepared milk chocolate frosting
soft-style peanut butter cookies
chocolate fudge pudding mix
angel food or pound cake

INDEX

FAVORITE RECIPES

Dotty Griffith is an award-winning food writer and editor with more than 15 years' newspaper experience. She has been food editor of The Dallas Morning News *for the past 10 years, and this is her second cookbook. She has edited two others. In addition, she has served as a judge for several national cooking contests, has been a regular guest host for the food section of a cable television show, and has served on the nutrition task force of the American Heart Association. She brings her enthusiasm for all types of food—but especially munchies—to this new book in the Barron's series.*

Many thanks to my wonderful kids, Kelly and Caitlin, for their tasting, their encouragement and their understanding about sharing Mom's time with this book. And, of course, special thanks to Prissy, without whose inspiration, suggestions and criticism, testing experience and patience, this book would never have been completed. Also, thanks to Cathy, Kim and Irene.